EXTREMELY
Embarrassing
Dad Jokes

Ian Allen

This edition published in the United Kingdom in 2015 by
Portico
1 Gower Street
London
WC1E 6HD

An imprint of Pavilion Books Company Ltd

ISBN 978-1-91023-208-8

A CIP catalogue record for this book is available from the
British Library.

10 9 8 7 6 5 4 3 2

Reproduction by ColourDepth
Printed and bound by Bookwell, Finland

This book can be ordered direct from the publisher
at www.pavilionbooks.com

EXTREMELY
Embarrassing
Dad Jokes

Ian Allen

PORTICO

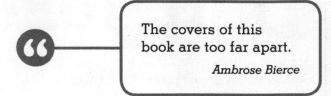

The covers of this
book are too far apart.

Ambrose Bierce

Hello again!

I'm delighted to bring you my third collection of brilliant Dad jokes. What I'm getting a bit fed up with, to be honest, is writing a new introduction every time. I asked my editor if I could just use one of the previous ones, on the grounds that no one ever reads them, and she said no.

Then I thought of my firstborn and his frequent assertions that he could do a better job of 'churning out that old rubbish' than me. So, bearing in mind the old adage of 'why have a dog and bark yourself?', I called his bluff. His credentials include acting as the test pilot for many of my jokes down the years, and being a history and philosophy student. And we all know what you say when you meet a philosophy graduate: 'Big Mac with fries, please.'

As with all students, his work was submitted late, therefore I haven't had a chance to read it myself, but I know how much he enjoys my jokes, so I feel sure it's in safe hands. So, without further ado, I give you ... Son of Dad.

Introduction

It's not easy being the son of one of Britain's leading joke-compilers – a title he's decided to bestow upon himself with, at best, limited evidence to substantiate it. All the fancy parties hosted by Hollywood stars and Nobel Prize-winning intellectuals; the constant stream of young women rushing up to him begging for an autograph; the paparazzi stalking my every move, desperate to catch the offspring of this colossal comic in an embarrassing situation to splash all over the tabloids. This must be how Jaden Smith feels.

Well, that may be a *slight* exaggeration. In fact, if I'm being honest, the only real impact my Dad's breakthrough into the embarrassing-dad-joke-book market has had upon me is that it's reinvigorated his efforts to pursue me and my siblings and fire off round after round of excruciating gags from his state-of-the-art machine pun. Oh God, now even *I'm* at it.

Back in 2011 when Dad first told me that he was compiling a joke book (*The Very Embarrassing Book of Dad Jokes*, which I've been forced, on pain of having some of its 'jokes' read aloud at my wedding, to remind you is still available on Amazon), my reaction was largely one of satisfaction that this bumbling old man was finally putting his uncanny ability to remember (and Google) awful jokes to good use.

One year later, however, he made the grand announcement over dinner one evening that he was working on a sequel (*Crap Dad Jokes*, also still available). This time, I was more concerned. Useless jokes had always just been an annoying but relatively harmless hobby, like bug-collecting or train-spotting. My Dad's relationship with jokes was becoming more serious. In fact, collecting and dispensing gags could now accurately be described as his job!

So, when he dropped the bombshell a few months ago that a shocking third book was in the pipeline, I had to take action. Enough is enough. I began to concoct an elaborate scheme, consisting mainly of fake sycophancy and embellished compliments, with the aim of convincing Dad to allow me some slim morsel of input into this historic threequel. Imagine my surprise, then, when *he* approached *me* to ask if I could write the entire introduction to the book! Well, I couldn't believe my luck! I was being handed on a silver platter a chance to directly warn the general public about Dad's latest Weapon of Mirth Destruction. Hiding my ecstatic disbelief, I humbly accepted his kind offer.

Here I am then, addressing you directly, before you've even read any of the jokes inside. I must now implore all the fathers of the world on behalf of all the children of the world: proceed with caution. The appalling jokes you're about to read will draw agonising groans and pained titters from those you love most. Marilyn Monroe once said, 'I don't mind making jokes, but I don't want to look like one.' Take it from one who knows, whose Dad has many times over-blurred that boundary of which the Blonde Bombshell spoke: your children won't necessarily find these gags as funny as you do, so maybe keep them to yourself, eh?

Chris Allen

> **A gravel lorry played a concrete lorry at football.**
>
> The gravel won on aggregate.

How many tickles does it take to make an octopus laugh?
Ten tickles.

Harriet: I think my chin is my best feature.
Horace: It looks to me like it's a double feature.

Patient: Doctor, my husband won't stop lying under the bed.
Doctor: It sounds as if he's a little potty.

Horace: I don't understand my wife.
Herbert: What's she done now?
Horace: I got in last night and there was a note on the fridge door: 'It's not working – I can't stand it any more – I'm leaving.' I opened the fridge, the light came on, the beer was cold ... I don't know what she was on about.

Visitor: Excuse me, what ward is Mr Smith in?
Nurse: The man run over by a steamroller? Wards 5, 6 and 7.

Teacher: Does anyone know what flatulence is?
Lucy: Is it what they take you to hospital in if you've been steamrollered?

Bobby: Mum, another kid thumped me on the way home.
Mum: That's awful – do you know who it was?
Bobby: No, but I've got his ear in my pocket.

If you go into the toilet American and come out of the toilet American, what are you while you're in the toilet?
European!

Son: What's Dad getting for his fiftieth birthday?
Mum: Bald and fat, by the look of it.

Dad's Daft Ditties
Hey diddle diddle, the cat and the fiddle,
The cow jumped over the moon,
The little dog laughed to see such fun,
And the cow burned up on re-entry.

Horace: Do you believe in free speech?
Herbert: Yes.
Horace: Good, lend me your phone.

Football captain: Why didn't you stop the ball?
Goalie: I thought that's what the net was for.

How much energy does it take to electrocute someone?
One killer-Watt.

How did the bald man keep his wig on?

With Airfix glue.

Tommy: Mummy, last night I saw the baby-sitter kissing a strange man in our living room.

Mum: What?!

Tommy: Ha-ha, April Fool … it was only Daddy.

A Yorkshireman and his wife went self-catering to Spain. When they arrived they realised they'd forgotten to pack the gravy to go with their pie. 'There's a British couple next door,' said the man, 'I'll pop round and see if they've got any.'

He knocked on the door and when the neighbour answered he asked, 'Hast any Bisto?'

'Sorry,' said the neighbour, 'I don't speak Spanish.'

Teacher: Who knows what a juggernaut is?

Sally: Is it an empty beer glass, miss?

Horace: You're cheating.

Herbert: How do you know?

Horace: You're not playing the cards I dealt you.

Judge: You shoplifted a tin of tomatoes, so I sentence you to four weeks in prison, one for each tomato.

Defendant's husband: Don't forget she also stole a tin of peas, your honour.

Why do pirates only get dangerous from the age of ten?

Because afore that they be nine.

A cow and a bull were in a field on the England-Scotland border – which one was Scottish?

The cow – she had her own bagpipes!

Patient: I'm having trouble breathing.

Doctor: Don't worry, I'll soon stop that.

> **What's white, has one horn and gives milk?**
>
> A milk lorry.

Teacher: Where were you born, Veronica?

Veronica: In Paris, sir.

Teacher: Really, why was that?

Veronica: I wanted to be near my mother.

DIY assistant: Can I help you, sir?

Man: I'd like a mouse trap, and please hurry, I've got a bus to catch.

Assistant: I don't think we've got one that big.

A lecturer of Ancient Greek took his trousers to be mended.

'Euripedes?' asked the tailor.

'Yes,' replied the lecturer. 'Eumenides?'

Horace: I'm making no money on my chip shop opening only one day a week.

Herbert: Why do you only open one day a week?

Horace: There's only one fry-day.

Horace: Me and the wife were walking down the riverbank the other day. She wanted to hold hands but I told her not to be stupid.

Herbert: Why, have you gone off her?

Horace: No, we were on opposite banks.

**The racehorse trainer was getting the horse
ready for the big race and giving the jockey his
instructions. He gave the horse something from
his bag and said to the jockey,**

'Now, take it steady for the first few furlongs, keep
out of trouble, then when you get to the mile post
really let it rip.'

**Just then the chief steward turned up and
interrupted. 'Excuse me, what was that you just
gave that horse?'**

'Oh,' said the trainer, 'it was just a sugar lump, look,'
and he popped one in his own mouth. 'Would you
like one?' He took another sugar lump from his bag
and gave it to the steward, who ate it.

'Thank you,' said the steward, 'carry on.'

'Right,' said the trainer when he'd left, 'like I said, let
him go at the mile post, and if anything passes you
after that, it'll either be me or the chief steward!'

What goes, 'I'm dreaming of a — KABOOM!!!'
Bang Crosby.

1 in 4 Dads thinks
Flickr is a horse.

Passenger: Will this bus get me to Regent Street?
Bus driver: Upper or Lower?
Passenger: All of me, you fool.

Horace: How was your fortnight in Wales?
Herbert: Not bad. It only rained twice – once for
seven days and the second time for a week.

**Sheila: While you're out, get some olives, and
some olive oil.**
Frank: I didn't know olives needed oiling.

Why do bears hibernate for so long?

Would you like to go in and wake one up?

> **Where's the best African country to be taken ill?**
>
> DR Congo.

Horace: I'm not feeling very well.
Herbert: Well you should take those mittens off.

Bobby: Did you see teacher throw that piece of chalk at Eric for copying my work?
Billy: Yes, he said it was a cheat-seeking missile.

Teacher: Why are you standing in the corner?
Jimmy: I'm trying to warm up – Mr Smith said corners were normally around ninety degrees.

Why did the farmer cross a chicken with an electric organ?
So he could have Hammond eggs.

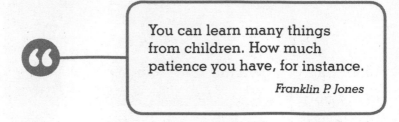

You can learn many things from children. How much patience you have, for instance.

Franklin P. Jones

Footballer: Would you send me off if I said you were a useless cheat?

Referee: Yes.

Footballer: But you couldn't send me off for thinking it?

Referee: No.

Footballer: Right then, I think you're a useless cheat.

What did the policeman say when he cut himself shaving?

I'm nicked!

Man: Can you give me something to cure fleas in my dog?

Vet: It depends on what's wrong with the fleas.

Horace: You look happy.

Herbert: The boss has just doubled my wages.
I used to get £100 a week, now he says he's going to pay me £100 every two weeks!

Horace: I'm going to change my bank.

Herbert: Why's that?

Horace: I went in yesterday and asked the lady if she'd check my balance, and she pushed me over!

> **What's brown, hairy, wears sunglasses and carries a stethoscope?**
>
> A coconut disguised as a doctor.

> **Terrible golfer: What do you think of my game?**
>
> Caddy: I think I prefer golf.

The vicar came to tea and Horace told a very
rude joke.

'How dare you tell that joke before me!' said
the vicar.

'I'm sorry, Reverend,' said Horace, 'you can
tell the next one.'

Horace and Herbert were fishing when the bailiff
arrived. As soon as he saw him, Horace threw his
rod down and started running as fast as he could.
The bailiff gave chase, and after a ten-minute
pursuit Horace stopped running and showed the
bailiff his fishing licence.

'Why did you run away if you've got a licence?'
asked the bailiff.

'I might have a licence,' said Horace, 'but Herbert
hasn't.'

Dad: What's all this arguing about?
Kids: We all want to play with the same toy.
Dad: Right, whoever never talks back to Mum and obeys her instantly can have it first.
Kids: OK, Dad, you can have it.

Patient: I keep having this awful dream. I'm in front of a door with writing on it, and I push and I push and I push but it won't open.
Doctor: What does the writing say?
Patient: 'Pull'.

Horace: Why did you punch your wife?
Herbert: It wasn't my fault, I asked what she wanted for her birthday and she said, 'A spa would be nice.'

What's invisible and makes funny clucking noises around your house?

A poultrygeist.

The old man was ill again, for the umpteenth time, and called for his wife to come to his bedside. As she sat by him, he whispered, 'Hilda, you've been with me all through the bad times. When I got fired, you were there to support me. When my business failed, you were there. When I had my car accident, you were by my side. When we lost the house, you stayed right here. When my health started failing, you were still by my side ... You know something, Hilda?'

'What, dear?' asked Hilda, her eyes brimming with tears.

'I'm beginning to think you're bad luck.'

What's a cannibal's favourite meal?

Snake and pygmy pie.

> **What do you give a stressed-out elephant?**
>
> Trunkquilisers!

Horace: I backed a horse in the two o'clock at Kempton at ten to one.

Herbert: What happened?

Horace: It came in at half-past four.

Horace: I had a text the other day and it said 'IDK'. What does that mean?

Harriet: I Don't Know.

Horace: No, neither did I.

Teacher: If a rooster lays an egg in the middle of a slanted roof, will it roll left or right?

Jimmy: Er, left, miss?

Teacher: No, you idiot – roosters don't lay eggs.

> **What guard has one hundred legs?**
>
> A sentry-pede!

Customer: I'd like a candle please.
Shopkeeper: Would you like a red one or a blue one?
Customer: Which burns longer?
Shopkeeper: Neither, they both burn shorter.

A vicar was walking down the street when he saw a little girl trying to reach a high-up knocker on a front door.
'Let me help,' he said, and knocked the door. 'Now, is there anything else I can do?'
'Yes,' said the girl. 'Now we run like hell!'

> **Where do ghosts go for a night out at Christmas?**
>
> The phantomime.

Why did the stupid Grand Prix driver make twenty-five pit stops?
He stopped once for fuel, twice for tyres and twenty-two times to ask for directions.

The bishop was visiting one of his vicars. 'Are you reading the Bible every day?' he asked.
'Certainly I am, your reverence,' said the vicar. 'I'll show you how well-thumbed it is. Mary,' he said to his four-year-old daughter, 'fetch that big book that Daddy's always reading.'
Mary returned with the Argos catalogue.

What are caterpillars afraid of?

Dog-erpillars.

Horace: I hate Halloween trick-or-treaters, so I turned all the lights off and pretended I wasn't in.
Herbert: Is that why you got the sack from the lighthouse?

What's the difference between a cat and a comma?
One has the paws before the claws, and the other has the clause before the pause.

Herbert: How's the wedding planning coming on?
Horace: We're having a slight difference of opinion; she wants a big church wedding, large reception, dance band, the works, and I want to elope with somebody else.

Horace: I like your new sundial.

Herbert: It's great, isn't it? And I've had floodlights installed so I can use it at night as well.

Son: What's the point of me learning a trade? There aren't any jobs.

Dad: Yes, but at least then we'd know what work you were out of.

Patient: Are these tablets addictive?

Doctor: Definitely not. I've been taking them myself for years.

Billy: You've got a funny nose.

Bobby: Well, I didn't pick it.

> **What does Speedy Gonzalez lay his carpets on?**
>
> Underlay, underlay!

Customer: Is that the pizza parlour?
Receptionist: Yes, what would you like?
Customer: Do you deliver?
Receptionist: No, just pizza.

Herbert was in the pub when Charlie came up and said he had a good trick. 'I'll put my hand by the wall and you thump it as hard as you can.' Just as Herbert's fist got to Charlie's hand he whipped it away and Herbert thumped the wall. **Herbert was walking home through the park when he met Horace and decided to try it out for himself.** 'Horace, I've got a great trick to show you. We really need a wall, but I'll just use my face for now...'

Waiter: Your bill, sir. Diner: I'm awfully sorry, but I've only just got enough money to pay this, and nothing for a tip. **Waiter: I might have made a mistake, sir – let me add it up again.**

Patient: I can't stop gloating all the time. Doctor: Have this cream, and *don't* rub it in.

Dad: Why don't you answer the phone?
Son: It's not ringing.
Dad: Trust you to leave everything to the last minute.

Interviewer: There are two things we value at this company – honesty and cleanliness. So, first question: did you wipe your feet on the doormat on the way in?
Candidate: Yes, I certainly did.
Interviewer: That's interesting, because we haven't got a doormat.

What has a bottom at the top?

Your legs.

Shaggy Dad Story #1

A monkey was dashing round the jungle, looking for something he'd lost. He asked every animal he met, 'Have you seen my little gadget, it's brilliant, it has four prongs on the end, it's ever so useful?'

He asked the lions and the tigers, the elephants and the crocodiles. He asked the snakes and the baboons and the wolves. But no one had seen it.

Finally he met a jaguar. 'Hello, jaguar, have you seen my little gadget, it's got four prongs on the end, it's ever so useful.'

'Yes,' the jaguar said. 'I've eaten it.'

'Eaten it!' screamed the monkey. 'Why?'

'Because I'm a four-point tool-eater jaguar.'

Herbert and Horace were on sentry duty in World War One.

Herbert said, 'You know we're on a bonus of sixpence for every German we capture?'

'Yes,' Horace said.

'Well, don't tell anyone else, but there's £500-worth coming over that hill.'

Jimmy was watching his mum put on face cream. 'What's that for?' he asked.

'It's to make me look beautiful,' she told him.

After a couple of minutes she started to wipe it off.

'Giving up already?' asked Jimmy.

Where do birds meet for coffee?

In a nest café.

> **Sally: How old is Granddad?**
>
> Sammy: I don't know but
> we've had him for ages.

Mum: How would you describe me?

Dad: ABCDEFGHIJK.

Mum: What do you mean?

Dad: Adorable, beautiful, cute, delightful,
elegant, funny, graceful, helpful, intelligent.

Mum: What about JK?

Dad: Just Kidding.

**Doctor: I'd advise you to give up drinking
and smoking.**

Patient: At my age, surely it's too late.

Doctor: It's never too late.

Patient: Well in that case there's no rush, is there?

Herbert: What are they calling your new grandson?

Horace: John.

Herbert: That's a bit of a common name – every Tom, Dick and Harry is called John.

Horace: How did you get that black eye?

Herbert: My wife asked me to get her favourite flower for her birthday but wouldn't tell me which it was. I took a guess and bought her some Homepride.

DAD STAT

Half of Dads weigh themselves *after* they've shaved (every little helps).

> **What's black and white and hangs from a line?**
>
> A drip-dry zebra.

Bertha: Why do you call your enormous knickers 'harvest festivals'?
Harriet: Because all is safely gathered in.

Horace: I see petrol's gone up again.
Herbert: It doesn't bother me – I always put in ten pounds' worth.

Horace: I was in the pub last night and a strange woman rolled her eyes at me.
Herbert: What did you do?
Horace: I picked 'em up and rolled 'em back.

Horace: You look puzzled, Herbert.
Herbert: I was just wondering, how come whenever I ring a wrong number it's never engaged?

Horace's father had died and Herbert went with
him to the funeral parlour to pay his respects.
'He looks very happy and peaceful,' said Herbert.
'Well, he died in his sleep, so he probably doesn't
know he's dead yet. When he wakes up the shock
will probably kill him.'

First person in pub: Have you seen that
ridiculous-looking girl dancing over there?
Second person: Do you mind, that's my *son*.
First person: I'm so sorry, I didn't realise
you were his father.
Second person: I'm his *mother*!

A man walked into a pub and said to the barman, 'Quick, give me a whisky before it gets started.'
'Before what gets started?'
'Never mind, just give me a whisky, quick!'
It sounded urgent so the barman gave him a drink. The customer downed it in one and said, 'Another, quick, before it gets started.'
'The barman gave him another whisky, but when he asked for a third one said, 'Hang on, when are you going to pay for these?'
'Oh, here we go,' said the customer, 'it's started.'

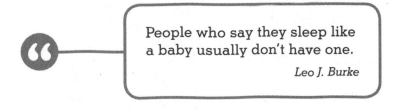

People who say they sleep like a baby usually don't have one.

Leo J. Burke

Sheila: My husband's got hundreds of people under him where he works.

Joyce: Your husband? Never!

Sheila: It's true, he's a gardener at the local cemetery.

Horace: I dropped my watch last night.

Herbert: Did it break?

Horace: No, luckily it fell on its hands.

Two men who overdosed on curry powder for a dare are in hospital. Now one's in a korma and the other's got a dodgy tikka.

Dad's Daft Ditties

There was a young man called Ed,
　　Had eyes in the back of his head.
When asked where he's going,
'I've no way of knowing,
　　But I know where I've been to,' he said.

> **What can a whole onion do that half an onion can't?**
>
> Look round!

Teacher: How many degrees in a circle?

Jimmy: It depends, sir.

Teacher: What on?

Jimmy: Do you want the answer in Fahrenheit or Celsius?

Dentist: I've got some good news and some bad news. The good news is that your teeth are fine.

Patient: What's the bad news?

Dentist: All your gums have got to come out.

> **What happened to the man who beat his bed to death?**
>
> He was charged with matricide.

> **How does an alien count to forty-six?**
>
> On its fingers.

Teacher: I thought I told you to stand at the end of the line.
Johnny: I tried but there was already somebody there.

Horace: Someone gave me a boomerang for Christmas, but I don't want it.
Herbert: Why don't you throw it away?
Horace: I've been trying to for the last fortnight!

Customer: I'd like to return this piano stool.
Music shop assistant: What's wrong with it?
Customer: I can't get a note out of it!

Dad: I've just made three cups of tea, put an odd number of sugar lumps in each one, and have used twenty sugar lumps. How?

Son: No idea.

Dad: I put one lump in each of two cups and eighteen in the other.

Son: Eighteen isn't an odd number.

Dad: It's an odd number of sugar lumps to put in a cup of tea.

Dad: Hello, love. Sorry I'm away at this business conference. Are you missing me?

Mum: Yes and no.

Dad: What do you mean?

Mum: Well, I'm so miserable it's almost as if you're still here.

What four-man American rock group doesn't sing or play?

Mount Rushmore!

Footballer: Why have you given a penalty, ref?
Referee: You just burped right into my face.
Footballer: Well, that should only be a freak hic.

Herbert: What's your life's ambition?
Horace: If I could live long enough to see my own
funeral, then I'd die happy.

What did Delaware?

Her New Jersey!

> **Why did the ant elope?**
>
> No one gnu.

A man was in hospital recovering from an operation when a nun came visiting. They got chatting about his family and he told her proudly of his wife and fourteen children.

'Fourteen children,' said the nun, 'what a good Catholic family. God is proud of you.'

'I'm sorry, sister, I'm not Catholic, I'm Anglican.'

'Anglican! And fourteen children! What are you, some kind of sex maniac?!'

Journalist: Congratulations on your 100th birthday. What's your secret?

Old man: I put it all down to slugs. I've never eaten one in my life.

Horace: My brother went to pieces when he went to jail.

Herbert: How do you mean?

Horace: He wouldn't shut up jabbering, took all his clothes off and broke all the furniture. We haven't played Monopoly since then.

Why did the world's first dating agency for chickens go bust?

They couldn't make hens meet!

Policeman: While I was undercover in the public house, the defendant came up to me and tried to pass four fifty-pound notes.

Lawyer: Counterfeit?

Policeman: Yes, she had two.

What's the definition of a transplant surgeon?

A man after your own heart.

Norman went mountain climbing, his rope broke and he ended up clinging to the cliff face by a thin branch. 'Is there anybody up there who can help me, anybody!' he shouted desperately.
Suddenly a voice spoke: 'NORMAN, THIS IS GOD. LET GO OF THE BRANCH AND I WILL SEE YOU LAND SAFELY.'
Norman was silent for a few seconds, and then said, 'Is there anybody else up there?'

What's purple, 5,000 miles long and full of pips?

The grape wall of China.

Frank and Sheila went shopping in Birmingham for the first time in twenty years. When they got there Frank suggested they split up.

'I'll ring you in a bit,' he told Sheila.

A couple of hours later he rang her. 'Where are you?' she asked.

'Well, do you remember when we came to Birmingham twenty years ago? And you saw that beautiful diamond bracelet but the kids were small and money was tight and we couldn't afford it. And I said that one day I'd come back and buy it, or something just like it, for you. Do you remember which jeweller's it was?'

'Oh, yes,' breathed Sheila.

'Well, I'm in the pub next door but I've run out of money. Can you come round and buy me another pint?'

Herbert: I've bought a great new clock. It goes eight days without winding.

Horace: And how long does it go if you wind it?

Herbert: What's the difference between a landline and a mobile phone?

Horace: Well, a landline is like a giant dog lying between two towns, and if you tread on his tail in one town he barks in the other.

Herbert: That makes sense – what about a mobile?

Horace: Well, a mobile is just the same, only without the dog.

What do you get if you cross the Atlantic with an accountant?

A Boring 747.

Horace: I thought you said this bucket you sold me was perfect – it's got a hole in it.

Herbert: I didn't say it was perfect, I said it was in mint condition.

Jimmy: I've just been round next door to see how Mrs Jones is, Mum.

Mum: That woman's a hypochondriac – I expect she thinks she's ill again.

Jimmy: No, today she thinks she's dead.

Patient: Doctor, I keep thinking I'm a bridge.

Doctor: What's come over you?

Patient: Seven cars, two buses and a lorry.

Diner: Waiter, your tie is in my soup.

Waiter: Don't worry, sir, it's washable.

What lives in America, has four
eyes and runs all day long?

The Mississippi.

Herbert is on his way home late at night when
he's attacked by a mugger. After a ferocious
fight, the mugger overcomes Herbert and
searches his pockets, but only finds a 50p piece.
'What sort of a nutter puts up a fight like that for
50p?' asks the mugger.
'I'm not that stupid,' says Herbert, 'I thought you
were after the fifty quid I've got hidden in my
shoe.'

Diner: I'll have a glass of water and a steak.
Waiter: Fillet?
Diner: Right to the top, please.

Herbert: Last week I fell in front of a moving train.

Horace: How did you survive that?

Herbert: It was going backwards.

Horace: I failed my entrance test for the SAS.

Herbert: What did you do?

Horace: I stormed a zoo and released all the ostriches.

Jimmy: I'd like a room for the night, please.

Hotel owner: I'm sorry, sir, we're full up.

Jimmy: I bet if the Queen turned up wanting a room, you'd find one for her.

Hotel owner: Yes, I suppose we would.

Jimmy: Well, she's not coming – I'll have her room.

Joyce: Times have changed, haven't they?

Sheila: I'll say. My kids have got so many expensive gadgets in their bedrooms, when they're naughty I have to send them to *my* room.

A train was approaching a station where Herbert, Harold and Horace were waiting on the platform.

'Here it comes,' said Herbert.

'No, here *she* comes,' said Horace.

'No, here *he* comes,' said Harold.

Harold was right, of course – it was a mail train.

Mum: Jimmy, why did you fall in that puddle with your new trousers?

Jimmy: I didn't have time to take them off.

Teacher: Bobby, why are you picking your nose in class?

Bobby: Cos I'm not allowed to at home, miss.

DAD STAT

4 out of 5 Dads confess to being delighted when hearing of other parents' sleepless nights.

Horace: I went to the doctor yesterday and he told me I had one buttock longer than the other.
Herbert: What a down right cheek!

Customer: A pint of bitter and a packet of helicopter crisps.
Barman: I'm sorry, we've only got plane crisps.

Why did the farmer feed his pigs one day and starve them the next?
He was trying to produce streaky bacon.

Patient: Doctor, I keep seeing frogs before my eyes.

Doctor: Don't worry, it's just a hoptical illusion.

Doctor: I've got some bad news and some good news.

Patient: Give me the bad news first.

Doctor: You're suffering from three different deadly diseases.

Patient: And the good news?

Doctor: I know how to cure two of them.

Herbert: Did you hear that Harold has died?

Horace: No! What did he die of?

Herbert: I'm not sure, but I don't think it was anything serious.

What's yellow and sneezes?

A banana with a cold.

Why did the farmer plough his field with a steamroller?

He was trying to grow mashed potatoes.

Horace: I got sacked from my job at the Samaritans because of a chap who rang up saying he was lying on the railway track waiting for a train.

Herbert: Why?

Horace: Apparently, 'Remain calm and stay on the line' was the wrong thing to say.

I have found the best way to give advice to children is to find out what they want and then advise them to do it.

Harry S. Truman

> **Horace: Why are you buying condensed milk?**
>
> Herbert: Well, I've only got a small fridge.

Herbert: My son was born on St George's Day, so we called him George.

Horace: That's funny, my son was born on St Patrick's Day, so we called him Patrick.

Harold: That's funny, that's exactly what we did with my son Pancake.

Horace: I think my wife's in for a letdown. She got all excited when I told her I was looking for cheap flights on the Internet.

Herbert: So?

Horace: Well, she's never taken much interest in my darts up to now.

Who was Admiral Horatio Nielson?

Admiral Nelson before he lost his eye.

Patient: What's that man doing hanging from your ceiling?

Psychiatrist: Oh, he's another patient – he thinks he's a light bulb.

Patient: Can't you cure him?

Psychiatrist: I could, but then I'd have to work in the dark.

Two men and a woman went for a job as an assassin with the CIA.

The first man was given a gun and told to go into a room and shoot the person sitting on the chair. He went in and came straight out again. 'That's my wife in there,' he said, 'I can't kill her.' So he was told he'd failed the test.

The second man was told the same thing, went into the room and came out after a minute. 'It was my wife,' he said, 'I just couldn't bring myself to pull the trigger.' He failed.

Finally the woman went in. She was in for five minutes, during which there was a loud commotion from the room. She finally came out breathless and dishevelled. 'You might have told me my husband was going to be in there,' she panted. 'And the stupid gun was full of blanks, so I had to beat him to death with the chair.'

> ### How was pasta invented?
> Someone used their noodle.

**A man went into a pub feeling low and said
to the barmaid, 'A pint, a pie and a few kind
words, please.'**
The barmaid poured him a pint and slapped a pie
in front of him without saying anything.
'What about the few kind words?' he pleaded.
'Don't eat the pie.'

**History teacher: Who knows what you have to
be to have a State funeral?**
Bobby: Dead, sir.

**Traveller: Can you tell me which is the latest
train back from London?**
Guard: Well, the 16:15 is usually later than any
of them.

A woman was in a plane next to a vicar when they went through a violent storm. Terrified, she said to him, 'Can't you do something?'

'Sorry, madam,' replied the priest, 'I'm in sales, not technical support.'

Teacher: Pay attention, Jimmy, here's a question. Sam's father had three children, he called the first two Snap and Crackle, what do you think he called the third?

Jimmy: Pop?

Teacher: No! Sam!

What happened to the greedy smash-and-grab robber?

They caught him when he went back for his brick.

Shaggy Dad Story #2

A bus conductor in Texas was on a final warning for his work, when one day he rang the bell for the bus to pull off while a little old lady was still trying to get on. She slipped under the wheels of the bus and was killed, and, this being Texas, the conductor was charged with murder, found guilty and sentenced to death in the electric chair.

Before his execution, he was given one last wish. 'I'd like a really green banana, please.'

He ate the banana, they threw the switch and nothing happened, so they set another date for his execution. Again, he asked for a green banana, ate it, the switch was thrown and nothing happened.

They set another date, checked everything out and tried again: green banana, switch, nothing.

'Well,' said the prison governor, 'we've tried three times, now we have to let you go. Just tell me, what was it with the green banana?'

'Nothing,' said the man, 'I'm just a really bad conductor.'

A man went parachuting for the first time. The instructor told him, 'Count to five and pull on the main chute; if that doesn't open, count to ten and pull on the reserve chute. Then you'll float slowly down to the ground and our truck will be there to drive you back to the airfield.'

The man jumped out, pulled the main chute – nothing happened. He pulled the reserve chute – nothing happened. He looked down at the fast-approaching ground and thought to himself: 'I bet that truck won't be there to pick me up either.'

> **Patient: Doctor, I think I'm a clock.**
>
> Doctor: Are you winding me up?

Dad: What's the difference between a terrorist and your Mum?
Son: I don't know.
Dad: You can negotiate with a terrorist.

Son: I'm not sure I want to use this glue stick.
Dad: Why not?
Son: It says, 'To use, take off the top and push up bottom.'

Dentist: That'll be ninety pounds.
Horace: OK, here's a cheque for your trouble.
Dentist: Oh, it's no trouble.
Horace: Wait till you try and cash the cheque.

Jimmy: My sister got married on Saturday and now she's got sixteen husbands.

Johnny: How do you mean?

Jimmy: Four richer, four poorer, four better and four worse.

Horace: Is that the fire brigade? My house is on fire.

999 operator: OK, how do we get there?

Horace: Haven't you still got those big red engines?

Horace: What's the secret of your long marriage?

Herbert: Well, we always make the effort to go out twice a week. A quiet restaurant, candlelit dinner, romantic music playing, a bit of dancing afterwards … I go Wednesdays and she goes Saturdays.

> They've finally got round to making a sequel to *ET*.
>
> It's called *ETC*.

Teacher: With what do we connect the name Baden-Powell?
Jimmy: With a hyphen, sir.

Headmaster: The standard of maths in this school is appalling.
Maths teacher: I know! Half my class don't know their times tables, half of them can't add up, and the other half can't even count!

Son: Thanks for lending me that money, Dad. I shall forever be in your debt.
Dad: That's what I'm afraid of.

What did the farmer say to the cow on his roof?

Get off my roof!

Herbert: Green side up, green side up, green side up, green side up, green side up...
Horace: What are you on about, Herbert?
Herbert: Don't distract me, I've got to get this turf home and laid before I forget the instructions.

England are priced at 20–1 to win the next World Cup.
For anyone who doesn't understand betting and odds, that means that if you bet twenty pounds you lose twenty pounds.

Why did the idiot give up fish-farming?

His tractor kept getting stuck in the river.

Fuzzy-wuzzy wuz a bear,
His name was Fuzzy-wuzzy,
But when Fuzzy-wuzzy lost his hair,
He wasn't fuzzy, wuz he?!

Car wash attendant: It's nice to see a Brummie now and again.

Horace: How did you know I was a Brummie?

Attendant: Well, we don't get many motorbikes riding through the machine.

Mum: Our kids do brighten up the home, don't they?

Dad: Well, they certainly never turn any flippin' lights off.

What's the best way to defeat your opponent?

Cut off his legs.

A policeman came across a young lad in a country lane next to a massive pile of hay that had obviously fallen off his cart. It was a hot day and the lad was sweating and straining trying to reload the hay.

'Why don't you wait for a tractor to come and help?' asked the policeman.

'My Dad wouldn't like it,' said the lad, working away.

'Well, at least stop and have ten minutes' rest.'

'No, my Dad wouldn't like it,' he repeated.

'Well, stop and have a quick drink from my water bottle,' said the copper.

'No, my Dad wouldn't like it.'

'Your Dad sounds like a right slave-driver, but he isn't here, is he?'

'Yes he is, he's under the hay.'

What do you give citrus fruit when it's poorly?

Lemon aid!

**When does Monday
come before Sunday?**

When you're reading
the dictionary.

**Horace and Herbert are watching a cowboy film
where John Wayne is galloping towards a fence.**
Horace says, 'I bet you a fiver he falls off when he
jumps the fence.'
'You're on,' says Herbert.
The Duke jumps the fence and, sure enough,
falls off.
**As Herbert is getting his money out, Horace
says, 'No, Herbert, I can't take your money,
I've seen this film before.'**
'Well, so have I,' replies Herbert, 'but I didn't think
John Wayne would make the same mistake twice.'

Horace: How's that electric car you bought?
Herbert: It's useless, I can't even take it off the drive – the lead only reaches 10 metres.

Teacher: Clive, put that chewing gum in the bin.
Clive: I can't do that, miss, my brother only lent it me for this morning.

Maths teacher: Who knows what a ratio is?
Jimmy: He's a sailor, sir.
Teacher: What do you mean, a sailor?
Jimmy: 'Oratio Nelson.

Cannibal chief: What's your job?
Victim in pot: I'm an editor.
Cannibal: Good news, you'll soon be editor-in-chief.

Horace: How did you get that flat tyre?
Herbert: I drove over a fork in the road.

Judge: I'm very disappointed. You were up before me two years ago for stealing a pair of shoes, and now here you are again on the same offence.

Defendant: You're right, your honour, they don't make shoes like they used to.

After a late night Horace and Herbert realised they'd missed the last bus back to Wolverhampton. As they were passing the bus depot, Horace suggested nipping in and 'borrowing' a bus to get them home.

Herbert kept lookout, and after half an hour and much revving of engines, Horace finally emerged at the wheel of a double-decker.

'What took you so long?' asked Herbert.

'It wasn't my fault,' said Horace, 'all the Wolverhampton buses were at the back.'

Horace: Our working men's club is looking for a treasurer.

Herbert: But I thought you hired one last month?

Horace: That's the one we're looking for.

Teacher: Who knows what a goblet is?

Jane: Is it a baby turkey?

Billy: My Mum and Dad bought me these rollerblades from Poundland.
Bobby: Cheapskates.

Horace and Herbert got jobs as demolition engineers and were on their way to bring down a block of flats.
'Mind those potholes, Herbert,' said Horace, 'there's a box of dynamite on the back seat.'
'Don't worry,' said Herbert, 'we've got a spare box in the boot.'

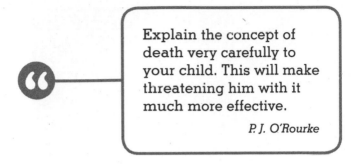

> Explain the concept of death very carefully to your child. This will make threatening him with it much more effective.
>
> *P. J. O'Rourke*

Horace: Cornet, please.

Ice cream man: Hundreds and thousands?

Horace: No, just one.

Did you hear about the snake who worked for the government?

He was a civil serpent.

A sailor was in his yacht off the German coast when it started taking in water. He got straight on the radio: 'Hello, coastguard, I'm sinking, I'm sinking!'

There was a pause of a few seconds before the coastguard spoke: 'OK ... Vat are you sinking about?'

Horace was trying to convince Herbert how intelligent his dog was. 'Pretend to shoot it,' he said.

So Herbert made a gun with his fingers, pointed them at the dog and said 'Bang!' The dog did nothing.

'See,' said Horace, 'he knew you were only pretending.'

Son: Dad, I need help with my homework. What happened to John Milton after he got married and then wrote *Paradise Lost*?

Dad: Well, from what I can remember, his wife died, and then he wrote *Paradise Regained*.

> **How do you get down from an elephant?**
>
> You don't, you get down from a duck!

Vicar: I always say a prayer before meals, Horace.
Horace: It sounds like your wife's cooking is as bad as mine, vicar.

Teacher: What is meant by a suspended sentence?
Bobby: Is it when they hang him, sir?

Horace: I sent my photo off to a Lonely Hearts column and they sent it back.
Herbert: Why?
Horace: They said no one was that lonely.

> **Wife: I've just been to the beauty parlour.**
>
> Husband: Was it shut?

Waiter: Would you like the fish hors d'oeuvres, sir?
Diner: I'll try the d'oeuvres – I'm allergic to fish.

Who drives round the West Country in a camper van?
Tess of the Dormobiles.

Teacher: What's wrong with your peas, Johnny?
Johnny: They're too hard, sir.
Teacher: Let me try some off your plate ... hmm, they don't seem *that* hard.
Johnny: No, but I've been chewing those for the last ten minutes.

Jimmy: Dad, the gas cooker's just gone out.
Dad: Well, relight it then.
Jimmy: I can't, it went out through the ceiling.

What does a triceratops sit on?

Its tricerabottom!

Herbert: My parrot lays square eggs.

Horace: Can it talk?

Herbert: It can only say one word – 'Ouch!'

Horace: I hate my wife's cat.

Herbert: Why?

Horace: It's always sitting in my chair. I put it outside, when I got back to my chair it was there. I drove it to the other side of town, chucked it out, when I got back it was in my chair. Finally I drove it to the middle of Wales and dumped it. An hour later I rang my wife.

Herbert: What did you say?

Horace: I said, 'Is the cat sitting in my chair?' She said it was. 'Put him on the phone,' I said. 'I'm lost.'

Mum: I've just tried to use that paper tablecloth you bought.
Dad: Was it any good?
Mum: No, it was tear-able.

Teacher: Who knows what 'centimetre' means?
Jane: When my Gran arrived on the train, Dad was centimetre.

Diner: Your Italian food is even better than the food I ate in Italy last month.
Chef: Of course. They have to use domestic cheese, ours is specially imported.

Herbert: This car you sold me is terrible. I thought you said it had one careful owner.
Salesman: I didn't say *all* its owners were careful.

Teacher: What's a bacteria?
Jimmy: The rear door to a cafeteria.

> ### Why has 'bird-cage' got a hyphen?
> For the budgie to perch on.

A man was walking on a beach when he found an old lamp. He gave it a rub and, of course, a genie appeared, promising to grant him one wish (he was a mean genie).

'Well, I've got relatives in Canada, but I hate flying. Please build me a bridge between England and Canada so I can visit them more often.'

The genie laughed. 'I'm sorry, that's impossible, even for me. The materials, construction problems, shipping lanes, it's out of the question. Have another wish.'

'Fair enough,' said the man. 'Well, I love football and it's always been my wish to see England win the World Cup.'

The genie thought for a minute then asked, 'How many lanes do you want on this bridge?'

Mum in chemists: Have you got any potties for my baby?

Assistant: No, I'm sorry, have you tried Boots?

Mum: Yes, but it comes out of the lace holes.

Mum: How did you get that flat tyre?

Dad: I ran over a milk bottle.

Mum: Didn't you see it?

Dad: No, the stupid milkman had it under his coat.

How did Mary and Joseph know how heavy Jesus was when he was born?

They had a weigh in a manger.

Why does a flamingo lift one foot off the floor?

Because if it lifted both feet it would fall over.

Dad's Daft Ditties

There once was a young lad named Clegm,
   Who couldn't get rid of his phlegm,
Ahegm, ahegm,
Ahegm, ahegm,
   Ahegm, ahegm, ahegm!

A man was returning to his seat in the theatre after a 'comfort break'.

'Excuse me,' he said to the lady by the aisle,
'did I step on your foot when I went out?'

'Yes, you did,' said the lady.

'Oh good, that means I'm in the right row.'

Jimmy: Dad, where are the Pyrenees?

Dad: I don't know, son, but I haven't had them.

> **What happens to ducklings when they grow up?**
>
> They grow down!

Mum: You told me you went to the pub to get the money Frank owed you, and you've come out without your glasses.
Dad: Yes, I went in optimistically, but came out misty optically.

Billy: Please, miss, how do you spell 'araphernalia'?
Teacher: Don't you mean 'paraphernalia'?
Billy: No, I've already written the 'P'.

Patient: I've just been stung on the finger by a bee.
Doctor: Oh dear, which one?
Patient: I don't know, all bees look the same to me.

> **What's blue and goes ding-dong?**
>
> An Avon lady trying to get out of a fridge.

What happened to the couple who met in a revolving door?
They've been going round together for ages.

Two men were on a building site, one weedy and little, one big and strong. The little chap said, 'I bet you twenty quid I can push something to the end of the yard in my wheelbarrow and you won't be able to push the same thing back.'
'You're on,' replied the big chap.
'Righto,' said the weed, 'jump in.'

8 per cent of Dads park right at the bottom of their drive to save petrol.

DAD STAT

A Red Indian chief had three wives. One slept on a buffalo skin, one on a bear skin and one on a hippopotamus skin. All the wives had babies: the buffalo wife had a boy, the bear wife had a girl, and the other had twins, one of each.

Which just goes to prove that the squaw on the hippopotamus is equal to the sum of the squaws on the other two hides!

Horace: I don't know whether to use a nail or a screw for this job.

Herbert: Well, use a nail, and if the wood splits you'll know you should have used a screw.

Horace: I surprised my wife with a Jaguar yesterday.

Herbert: That's a bit extravagant.

Horace: Well, they hadn't got any lions left.

Barber: Can I check, were you wearing a red scarf when you came in?

Customer: No.

Barber: Then I've just cut your throat.

What do angry mice send one another in winter?

Cross-mouse cards.

Sally: I'm glad I wasn't born in Russia, miss.

Teacher: Why, Sally?

Sally: Because I can't speak Russian.

How can you tell when witches are carrying a time bomb?

You can hear their brooms tick.

What was the most amazing thing they discovered when they found the wreck of the *Titanic*?

After over a hundred years, the swimming pool was still full.

What did the musician who played a rubber trombone do?

He joined an elastic band.

Who killed Dracula with a sausage roll?

Buffet the vampire-slayer.

> **What do you call a man stuck between two buildings?**
>
> Ali.

A circus was holding auditions and a ninety-year-old man turned up.

'What do you do?' asked the ringmaster.

'I bend over backwards and pick up a handkerchief off the floor with my teeth.'

'Wow, then what do you do?'

'Then I bend over again and pick up my teeth.'

Horace: I've just come out of Poundland with four suits for a quid.

Herbert: How did you manage that?

Horace: I bought a pack of cards.

If a man was born in Scotland, lived in Wales and died in England, what would he be?

Dead.

> **What did the worm say to the caterpillar?**
>
> Where did you get that fur coat?

Sheila: My husband has a great personality.
Joyce: Yes, mine's ugly too.

Boss: Why are you late, Perkins?
Perkins: I overslept.
Boss: You mean you sleep at home as well?

Teacher: What is it called when two people sing at the same time?
Susan: A duel, miss.

Horace: I'm fed up with being called Horace Smellie, I'm going to change it.
Herbert: Good idea, what to?
Horace: Well, I think Howard Smellie sounds quite nice.

A man thinks his wife is getting hard of hearing but she won't admit it. So he decides to test his theory once and for all. That evening, she's at the sink in the kitchen.

He stands about six paces behind her and asks, 'What's for tea, dear?'

No answer.

He moves a couple of paces closer and repeats the question. No response.

So he moves right to his wife's shoulder and again asks, 'What's for tea, dear?'

At this, his wife turns round and says, 'For the *third* time, sausages!'

Why does Rudolf have a red nose and all the other reindeer have brown ones?

Rudolf's the only one whose brakes work.

> ᗯhat do you call a day that follows two days of rain?
>
> Monday.

> **What did St Peter say when Joan of Arc arrived at the Pearly Gates?**
>
> Well done!

Herbert: I gave the postman a shock today – I went to the door naked.

Horace: He must have seen stuff like that before.

Herbert: Yes, but he was surprised that I knew where he lived.

A footballer was getting out of his Bentley when another car zoomed past and ripped the car door clean off. When the police arrived the footballer was still moaning about the damage to his car.

The policeman said, 'Sir, never mind your precious car, don't you realise your left arm was torn off in the accident?'

The footballer looked at the stump where his arm used to be and yelled, 'Nooooooooooo! My Rolex!'

A traffic policeman stopped a car that was trundling slowly along the M25 and asked him, 'Why are you going so slowly, sir? You're holding up traffic.'

'Well,' replied the motorist, 'the signs say "25".'

'But that's just the road number, not the speed limit,' said the copper. Then he noticed that a woman in the back seat was trembling all over. 'Is your passenger all right, sir?'

'Don't worry, officer,' said the motorist, 'my wife's always like that when we come off the A127.'

Harriet (on phone): Hello, Horace, the car won't start, the engine's damp.

Horace: How do you know it's damp?

Harriet: Because I've driven into the canal.

What's red and bad for your teeth?

A brick.

Horace: You're late, where have you been?

Herbert: I've just buried my mother-in-law.

Horace: What are all those cuts and bruises?

Herbert: Well, she put up a hell of a fight.

Doctor: Stop worrying about your health. You'll live to be eighty.

Patient: I am eighty!

Doctor: What did I tell you!

Teacher: Which month has twenty-eight days?

Billy: All of them, sir.

Shaggy Dad Story #3

An old lady decided to get a parrot to keep her company. She took it home in its little cage and was ever so pleased for a few days, but it wouldn't speak.

She went back to the pet shop and the owner suggested she buy a little ladder to give it some exercise. She did this, and it hopped up and down the ladder, but still didn't talk.

So she went back to the shop and the owner suggested the parrot might need a bit of stimulus, so she bought a little bell it could ring and a ball to push around. The parrot used the new toys, but still said nothing.

So the old lady went back to the shop and on the owner's advice bought a little mirror, in case the parrot wanted to see what it looked like, but that didn't work either.

The old lady went back to the shop and the owner said he'd tried everything and maybe it was just a non-talking parrot. Disappointed, the old lady went back home and found the parrot lying in the bottom of the cage, obviously on its last legs. And with its dying breath, the parrot said…

'…Doesn't that flippin' pet shop sell bird seed!'

Dad's Daft Ditties

There was a young curate from Kew
    Who kept a small cat in a pew,
He taught it to speak
Alphabetical Greek
    But it never got further than μ.

Herbert: I'm fed up with my wife.
Horace: Why?
Herbert: She texted me last night to say she was in Casualty. I watched the whole episode and never saw her once. She still hasn't come home.

Why did the man try to gatecrash a party dressed as a pirate and a shepherd?
He was going to get in by hook or by crook!

What's a Freudian slip?

It's when you say one thing and mean a mother.

Politician: I'm thinking of going on a charm offensive.

Spin-doctor: Well, you're halfway there already.

Politician: You mean I'm fifty per cent charming?

Spin-doctor: No, you're a hundred per cent offensive.

Horace: Are you there, Lord?

God: I'm always here. What do you want to know?

Horace: Is it true that to you a million years is like a second and a million pounds is like a penny?

God: Yes.

Horace: Can you lend me a penny?

God: OK, in a second.

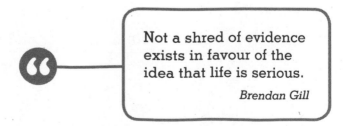

Not a shred of evidence exists in favour of the idea that life is serious.

Brendan Gill

> ## What did Sigmund Freud say came between fear and sex?
>
> Funf.

A young policeman came off his first late shift and was surprised to be given a bag of blue crystals by his boss.

'What's this?' he asked.

'It's the copper nitrate.'

Horace: My wife said she wanted me to buy her something that will go from 0 to 200 in a few seconds.

Herbert: That sounds expensive, what have you bought her?

Horace: A set of bathroom scales.

Patient: Doctor, I think I'm a famous psychoanalyst.

Doctor: How long has this been going on?

Patient: Ever since I was Jung.

A young sea cadet was being tested by an examiner.

Examiner: Suppose you're at sea and a storm comes up?

Cadet: I'd toss out an anchor.

Examiner: And what if another storm came in?

Cadet: I'd toss out another anchor.

Examiner: But what if an even bigger storm arose?

Cadet: I'd toss out another anchor.

Examiner: Ah, but tell me — where are you getting all your anchors from?

Cadet: The same place you're getting your storms.

> ### Do zombies like being dead?
> Of corpse they do.

Horace: I see Stephen Hawking has finally written a new book about something or other.
Herbert: Well, it's about time.

Dad: I'm worried I'm going to lose my job. A company has invented a gadget that does everything I do, but quicker and better.
Mum: Do you know where I can buy one?

> ## Where do fish keep their money?
> In the riverbank.

Mum: We've been married twenty years – how old do you think I look? Be honest!
Dad: Well, from your skin I'd say twenty-eight, from your hair, twenty-five, from your figure, twenty-nine.
Mum: Oh, what a lovely thing to say.
Dad: Hang on, I haven't finished adding it up yet.

'This is your captain speaking ... AND THIS IS YOUR CAPTAIN SHOUTING!'

Patient: Dr Finlay, whenever I eat chocolate and coconut it gives me stomach ache.
Dr Finlay: Och, it's boun' tae.

Interviewer: If you got the job as zoo keeper, what steps would you take if the lions escaped?
Horace: Great big ones!

Dad's Daft Dictionary

Alarm clock: device to wake up people
  who don't have children.

Circular definition: see Definition, circular.

Definition, circular: see Circular definition.

Politician: someone who enters a revolving door
  behind you and comes out in front of you.

Teacher: one who talks in someone else's sleep.

And if Dad was in charge of the dictionary ...

... haemorrhoids would be called ass-teroids.

... OCD would be renamed CDO – in
  nice, neat alphabetical order.

... dyslexia wouldn't be so hard to spell.

... lisp wouldn't have an 's' in it.

> **Horace: I'd go to hell and back for you, darling.**
>
> Harriet: Oh, you don't have to come back just for me.

Patient: I'm feeling a little down in the mouth.
Doctor: Well, next time make sure you pluck your goose before you eat it.

Horace: I've been thinking about rising sea levels.
Herbert: What about them?
Horace: Well, just think how much higher it would be if there weren't any sponges in the sea.

22 per cent of Dads know their personal best time of mowing the lawn to the second.

DAD STAT

Jimmy: What does your Dad do?
Johnny: He's an MP.
Jimmy: Wow! Honest?
Johnny: No, just the normal sort.

Horace: My wife bet me I couldn't make a car out of spaghetti.
Herbert: What happened?
Horace: Well, you should have seen her face when I drove pasta.

Horace: I've heard that outside of a dog, a book is a man's best friend.
Herbert: And inside of a dog, it's too dark to read.

Horace: Why are you looking so pleased?

Herbert: After having six daughters my wife finally had a little boy last week.

Horace: Congratulations! Does he look much like you?

Herbert: To tell the truth I haven't looked at his face yet.

First scientist: I've just discovered a faster-than-light particle.

Second scientist: I bet you didn't see that coming.

How do you get a one-armed idiot out of a tree?

Give him a wave.

Teacher: What is a fortification, Tommy?

Tommy: Is it two twentyfications?

> **Where does a sick ship go?**
> To the dock.

Billy: I just asked Dad a question about astronomy and he whacked me.
Sally: What did you say?
Billy: All I asked him was, 'Is Uranus bigger than Mars?'

What's the difference between a magician and an experimental psychologist?
One pulls rabbits out of hats, the other pulls habits out of rats.

Patient: Doctor, I keep thinking I'm a small bucket.
Doctor: You do look a little pale.

Johnny: Mum, can I play with Granddad?
Mum: No, you've dug him up twice this week already.

Horace: I've just auditioned for *Snow White and the Seven Dwarfs*.
Herbert: Did you get the part?
Horace: I don't know, but I'm on the short list.

Susan: Just how stupid is Dad?
Mum: Put it this way, if brains were dynamite he wouldn't have enough to blow his nose.

Horace: Why are you crying, love?
Harriet: I'm homesick.
Horace: But this is your home.
Harriet: I know, and I'm sick of it!

What did Columbus ask when he went to buy a new ship?
How many miles to the galleon does it do?

Time flies like an arrow —
fruit flies like a banana.

Patient: Doctor, I've been coughing for a month and nothing you've done has helped.
Doctor: Right, I'm going to give you a massive dose of laxative.
Patient: Will that cure my cough?
Doctor: Put it this way, you won't dare to.

Horace: The food at our last OAP meeting was terrible.
Herbert: Well, you should bring it up at the next one.

Sergeant: Who knows what a Royal Enfield is?
Private: Is it where the Queen keeps her chickens?

An MP is visiting the local mental asylum. 'How do you decide whether to commit someone?' he asks.

'Well,' says the director, 'we fill up a bath with water, then give the patient a teaspoon, a mug and a bucket and ask them to empty the bath as quickly as possible.'

'I see,' says the MP, 'and if he's got any sense he'll choose the bucket.'

'No,' says the director, 'if he's got any sense he'll pull the plug out. Would you like a bed next to the window with a view?'

What happened when there was an explosion in a French cheese factory?

All that was left was de brie.

What did Jason Orange do when he got beaten up?

Joined Pulp.

What's an orchestra conductor's favourite game?

Haydn seek!

Horace: I had to get up at four o'clock this morning to answer the door in my pyjamas.
Herbert: Why on earth have you got a door in your pyjamas?

Daddy Bear: Who's eaten my porridge?
Baby Bear: Who's eaten my porridge?
Mummy Bear: Will you two shut up and give me a chance to *make* the flippin' porridge!

What's a horse's favourite sort of food?

Oat cuisine.

Herbert and Horace were on a plane to New York when the captain came on the intercom. 'I'm afraid one of our four engines has failed, there's no danger, but we will be an hour late arriving in New York.'

Half an hour he came on again: 'Very sorry, but a second engine has failed. Still no problem, but we will be two hours late in New York.'

An hour further on the captain spoke again: 'Please don't worry, the third engine has failed. We'll be all right, but we will be three hours late in New York.'

At this Herbert turned to Horace and said, 'Let's hope the fourth engine doesn't fail, or we'll be up here all night!'

Dad's Daft Ditties

Humpty Dumpty sat on a wall,
   Humpty Dumpty had a great fall,
All the King's horses and all the King's men
   Said, 'Scrambled eggs for breakfast again!'

7 per cent of Dads are so thrifty they cut the top off a toothpaste tube with scissors to get at the last little bit.

Son: Why does Dad's face look like that?

Mum: Well, my theory is that when God was giving out noses your Dad thought he said 'roses' and asked for a big red one. Then when he was giving out chins he thought he said 'gins' and asked for a double.

Optician: You need glasses.

Patient: How do you know without examining me?

Optician: It was something about the way you came in through the window.

What do clouds wear under their trousers?

Thunderpants!

Dad: Sorry to ring you, love, but I've locked my keys in the convertible – can you bring the spare set?

Mum: I'll be with you in twenty minutes.

Dad: Well, hurry up – the top's down and it's starting to rain.

Policeman: Are you the driver of this one-man bus, sir?

Driver: Yes, officer.

Policeman: And what happened when the bus crashed?

Driver: I haven't got a clue, I was upstairs collecting the fares at the time.

How do you organise a space party?

Planet!

> ### How do you make an idiot laugh on Saturday?
>
> Tell him a joke on Wednesday.

Woman: Doctor, is there any hope for my husband?
Doctor: That depends on what you're hoping for.

Herbert: I hear you had all your teeth taken out at the dentist.
Horace: I did. I tell you what, though, never again!

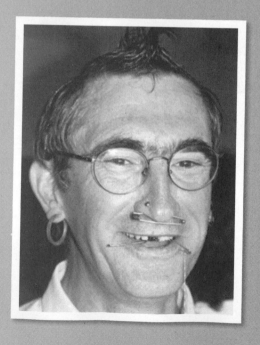

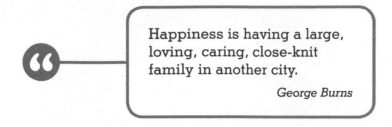

> Happiness is having a large, loving, caring, close-knit family in another city.
>
> *George Burns*

Billy: Miss, how long can someone live without a brain?
Teacher: I'm not sure, Billy, how old are you?

Joyce: Your hubby's put on weight, hasn't he?
Sheila: I'll say – the only thing from his wedding outfit that still fits is the tie.

Why did the statistician always take a bomb with him when he travelled by plane?
He knew the chances of one bomb being on a flight was one in a million, and therefore that the chances of *two* bombs being on board was one in a million million.

> **What happened to the Eskimo who sat on the ice all day?**
>
> He got Polaroids.

Horace: I'm sorry, Herbert, I've just run over your cat. Can I replace it?
Herbert: That depends how good you are at catching mice.

Woman: Doctor, my husband thinks he's a parachute.
Doctor: Tell him to drop in and see me.

Herbert: I bought one of those rocket lettuces the other day.
Horace: Was it nice?
Herbert: I don't know, it went off before I could eat it.

A man was sitting on a park bench next to a screaming child in a pushchair. He kept repeating quietly, 'Jack, don't worry, calm down, everything will be OK, you'll be feeling better eventually, I promise,' over and over and over again.

A woman was passing and stopped by the bench. 'Can I just say how lovely it is to see you being so patient and calm – Jack is very lucky to have a Dad like you.'

'Thank you, madam,' said the man, 'but I'm Jack!'

A man answered a knock on the door to find a snail on the doorstep. He picked up the snail and threw it as far as he could.

Two years later he answered another knock on the door and there was a snail on the doorstep again. The snail said, 'Why did you do that?'

Why don't giraffes eat very much?

Because a little goes a long way.

Horace: A pile of books fell on my head yesterday.

Herbert: You ought to sue someone.

Horace: No, I've only got my shelf to blame.

Horace: I've just had a lady from Eastern Europe clean my house. It took her four hours to hoover the carpets.

Herbert: It sounds like she was a Slovak.

Herbert: This furniture goes back to Louis the Fourteenth.

Horace: Really?

Herbert: Yes, unless we pay Louis by the Thirteenth.

Where do frogs fly their flags?

On tadpoles.

What is a teacup?

Nineteen sizes up on an A-cup.

Dinner guest: Why is your dog looking at me like that?

Host: Don't worry, he just doesn't like you using his plate.

Teacher: What can you tell me about a motorcycle with 250 cubic centilitres?

Jimmy: It was made in Cuba.

What happened to the man who tried to pick up too many boxes of colanders?

He strained his muscles!

Policeman: Did you see the vehicle that hit you?

Man: No, but I know it was my mother-in-law driving – I'd recognise that laugh anywhere.

Horace and Herbert went into a pub and started playing pool. After an hour neither had potted a ball.

'Horace,' said Herbert, 'let's cheat and take that wooden frame off.'

Horace: Did you sign up for that online account?

Herbert: No, it wouldn't let me. It kept asking me to choose a password with eight characters including a number.

Horace: So what was the problem?

Herbert: Well, no matter how many times I typed in 'Snow White and the Seven Dwarfs' it wouldn't accept it.

What did the pirate say on his eightieth birthday?

Aye, Matey!

Woman: Is that 999? Two men are fighting over me.

Operator: And what's the emergency?

Woman: The ugly one's winning.

Captain: You've done very well, private – how would you like a commission?

Private: If it's all the same to you, sir, I'd rather just have a bigger salary.

Patient: Doctor, can you give me anything for my halitosis?

Doctor: Take a spoonful of horse manure twice a day.

Patient: Will that cure it?

Doctor: No, but it'll take the edge off the smell.

> **What do you do with a tree after you chop it down?**
>
> Chop it up!

Dad: You really upset me when you called me stupid.

Mum: I'm sorry, I thought you already knew.

Two nuns are driving down a narrow country lane when they meet a drunk weaving across the road in front of them. They drive right up to him, rev the engine, toot the horn, but he won't move out of the way.

Then one nun has an idea. 'Sister Maria, why don't you show him your cross.'

So Sister Maria wound down the window and shouted, 'Get out of the flaming way, you drunken old reprobate!'

What happens when the Pope dies?

Another Popes up.

Did you hear about the drummer who decided to kill himself because his timing was so bad?
He threw himself behind a train.

Horace: Have you ever thought about doing voluntary work?
Herbert: I wouldn't do it if you paid me!

Judge: You have been found guilty of the attempted murder of your mother-in-law, but I will give you a suspended sentence.
Defendant: Thank you for giving me a second chance, your honour.

32 per cent of Dads can't remember their kids' birthdays without writing them down.

DAD STAT

Woodwork teacher: What are you making, Billy?

Billy: A portable, sir.

Teacher: A portable what?

Billy: I don't know yet, I've only made the handle.

Horace: The doctor put me on a diet of coconuts and bananas.

Herbert: Have you lost much weight?

Horace: No, but you should see me climb a tree.

Mum: Now you've had a promotion you can buy a new hat.

Dad: No, I don't want success to go to my head.

Shaggy Dad Story #4

A Roman galley packed with slaves chained to the oars was making its way through the Mediterranean. Another enormous slave was beating out time on a huge gong at the front of the ship. The trouble was, the ship was so long that the slaves at the back couldn't hear the gong in time and kept rowing out of time. Every time they did this they got whipped.

That night they decided to do something about it. A few of them managed to slip out of their chains and they went to move the gong to the middle of the ship so everyone could hear it at the same time. The only trouble was, it was so enormous and heavy they couldn't budge it. They could just about rock it.

Then one had an idea. He got a load of grease and persuaded the massive slave who kept time to lie down on his back – then he plastered his chest with grease. They managed to tip the gong on to him and started to slide it slowly towards the centre of the ship.

Just then the slave master returned unexpectedly. He took one look at the scene and shouted, '*Lorem quid putas in terris*?!' ('What on earth do you think you're doing?'). The slaves all turned to him and sang:

'We're rolling a gong on the chest of a slave...'

> **What's worse than when it's raining cats and dogs?**
>
> Hailing taxis.

Two Aussie blokes are hiking in the Australian outback when one is bitten on the bum by a rattlesnake. Luckily the other has a satellite phone, and he calls for the flying doctor.

'Listen,' says the doctor, 'I can't get to you for an hour – if you don't suck the poison out in the next ten minutes your friend will die.'

'What did he say?' asks the victim.

'Mate, he says you're going to die.'

Did you know the Lone Ranger has a cousin in Manchester who's a florist?

He's the Hyde Ranger.

Judge: You have been found not guilty of theft and are free to go.

Defendant: Great! Can I keep the diamonds as well?

Horace: I worry that you only want to marry me because my father left me a fortune.

Harriet: Don't be silly. I'd want to marry you whoever had left you a fortune.

Diner: I've been waiting here for half an hour, it's a disgrace.

Waiter: How do you think I feel, I've been waiting here for six years!

What do you call shoes made out of banana skins?

Slippers.

How much does a cockney pay for shampoo?

Pantene!

First dog: I've noticed you only wee up lamp-posts and avoid the parking meters. Second dog: Well, have you seen how much they charge?

A persistent vacuum-cleaner salesman lured his way into Sheila's house. He wouldn't take no for an answer. He tipped a container of dust and ash over the carpet and announced, 'If my machine doesn't get every bit of that up, I'll eat it myself.' 'I'll go and get you a spoon,' said Sheila, 'they've just cut our electric off.'

Horace: It's a good job that time exists, isn't it?
Herbert: How do you mean?
Horace: Well, otherwise everything would happen all at once.

Horace: I've just spilled stain remover on my shirt.
Herbert: Oh, you'll never get that out.

Why did the man sprinkle weedkiller on his laptop?

He wanted to make it fuchsia-proof.

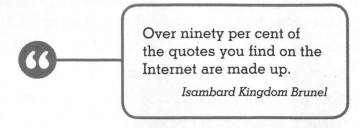

Over ninety per cent of the quotes you find on the Internet are made up.

Isambard Kingdom Brunel

Policeman: Good evening, sir, we're looking for a man with an ear trumpet.
Herbert: Wouldn't you do better using binoculars?

Horace: I met my wife in a dance hall.
Herbert: What was the first thing you said to her?
Horace: I said, 'I thought you were at home looking after the kids.'

Comedian: I feel a bit funny tonight.
Manager: Well get out there quick before it wears off.

Sally: What's wrong? You've just been given a huge diamond ring.

Sarah: But with the ring comes the terrible curse of the Fotheringays.

Sally: And what's that?

Sarah: Horace Fotheringay.

Horace: Did you see that terrible ventriloquist on *Britain's Got Talent* last night?

Herbert: Yes, he was so bad his lips moved even when he wasn't talking.

Horace: I'm packing in my job as a human cannonball.

Herbert: That's a shame – where are they going to find someone of your calibre?

Why did the cat hijack a plane?

He wanted to go to the Canaries.

43 per cent of Dads think Cillit Bang is a Danish footballer.

Horace: I've just been to that new farm shop – it was a bit smelly.
Herbert: Yes, I really don't know why the sewage farm bothers with one.

Horace: I asked your wife how old she was and she said she was approaching fifty.
Herbert: Yes, but she didn't say from which direction.

Sheila: Why do you call your husband 'Nature'?
Joyce: Because he abhors a vacuum.

What are the most beautiful valleys?

The ones that are gorges!

> ### How do you mend a broken crab?
> With crab paste.

Horace: Gavin died last week, he had terrible heartburn and swallowed too much medicine.
Herbert: You mean Gav is gone?

Who was the last person to box Rocky Marciano?
His undertaker.

Coroner: Do you remember your husband's last words?
Widow: Yes, he said, how on earth can the butcher make any money selling meat that cheap?

Customer: I'd like to buy a watch, please.
Jeweller: Certainly, sir, analogue?
Customer: No, just a watch.

An old man, a professional footballer and a boy scout were up in an old plane for a tourist flight around the bay. After a few minutes the pilot had a heart attack; just before he died he managed to splutter, 'There are two parachutes over there ... good luck.'

Before they could discuss how to divide two parachutes between three people, the footballer grabbed hold of the straps of the package next to him and jumped out of the plane.

Shocked, the old man said, 'Well, I've had my time, lad. You take the other parachute.'

'We'll both be OK,' said the boy scout. 'The footballer just jumped out with my rucksack.'

What's the difference between your first baby and your last baby?

You sterilise the first one's dummy by boiling it and the last one's by blowing on it.

Customer: Is it right you specialise in hard-to-find books?

Shopkeeper: That's right.

Customer: Have you got *Fly Fishing* by J.R. Hartley?

Shopkeeper: I don't know, why don't you try and find it.

Nan: Johnny, you shouldn't pull funny faces. When I was little I was told if I pulled funny faces and the wind changed I'd stick like it.

Johnny: Well, you can't say you weren't warned.

Patient: So, how do I stand, doctor?

Doctor: That's what puzzles me.

> **What did Jay-Z call his wife before they got married?**
>
> Feyoncé!

Horace: I was so unpopular at school they used to call me 'Batteries'.

Herbert: Why?

Horace: Because I was never included in anything.

Why did the sergeant assault his recruits with pepper spray and mustard gas?

He wanted them to become seasoned veterans.

Horace: What's the best thing about Switzerland, do you reckon?

Herbert: Well, the flag is a big plus ...

Horace: Did you get that job at the hotel?

Herbert: No, it turned out when they said they wanted 'inn-experienced' people I wasn't what they had in mind.

The Sadler's Wells Ballet played the Bolshoi Ballet at football yesterday.

It ended 2–2.

Frank: Will you take this ring and marry me?

Sheila: Gosh, are they real diamonds?

Frank: I hope so, or I've just been diddled out of a tenner.

Horace: My Granddad died when he fell through a trapdoor and broke his neck.

Herbert: Was there anyone with him?

Horace: Just the hangman.

How do snails keep their shells so shiny?

Snail varnish.

A Yorkshireman's wife died and he asked the stonemason to put a simple inscription on her headstone: 'She was thine'. But when he went to inspect the work, it said, 'She was thin'.

'You daft beggar, you've missed off the "e",' he complained. The stonemason said he'd put it right for the next day.

Sure enough, when the man returned the next day the stone read: 'Ee, She was thin'.

Diner: What's this dirty, brown stuff? I asked for still water.

Waiter: It might be dirty and brown but it's still water.

Who's afraid of Virginia Woolf?

Virginia Sheeep!

Dad's Daft Ditties

I eat my peas with honey,
   I've done it all my life,
It makes the peas taste funny,
   But it keeps them on the knife!

Horace: Is Herbert in?

Herbert's wife: I'm afraid he died last night.

Horace: Oh dear ... he didn't happen to mention that tenner he owed me, did he?

What do you get if you cross a hyena with a man-eating tiger?

I don't know.

Neither do I, but if it laughs you'd better join in.

What do you call a caveman with no sense of purpose?

A meanderthal!

Teacher: Complete the saying, 'Those who live by the sword ...'
Johnny: Get shot by those who live by the gun.

Horace: I showed my doctor a rash on my bum yesterday and he was all embarrassed and uncomfortable.
Herbert: That's very unprofessional, what did he say?
Horace: He told me to make an appointment like everyone else and said he was never going to shop in Aldi again.

Why are prisoners called jailbirds?

Because they've been robin.

DAD STAT

12 per cent of Dads can't remember all their kids' middle names.

Mr Robinson went on holiday and found himself at the hotel breakfast table every morning with a Frenchman. On the first morning before eating the Frenchman said, 'Bon appetit.' 'Robinson,' replied the Englishman.

The same occurred every morning, until one day after breakfast a waiter mentioned to the Englishman that the Frenchman was merely wishing him a good meal.

The next morning, before his companion could say anything, Robinson said confidently, 'Bon appetit.'

'Robinson,' replied the Frenchman.

Horace: My Granddad's a hundred today!
Herbert: That's nothing, if my granddad was still alive he'd be 125.

First drunk: Haven't I met you before in Newcastle?
Second drunk: Nope, I've never been to Newcastle.
First drunk: Me neither, it must have been two other blokes.

Vicar: I couldn't help noticing that your husband walked out of my sermon this morning.
Mrs Smith: It was nothing personal, vicar. He's been walking in his sleep for years.

A man was walking through his local park when he saw two council workers. One would dig a hole, move on a few feet, dig another one, and so on. The other was following him, filling in all the holes he'd dug.

The man was furious. He stormed up to the workers, saying, 'I'm going to write to the council, all this digging holes and filling them in again, it's a disgrace.'

'Hang on,' said the filler-in. 'It's not our fault that Charlie's off sick.'

'Who's Charlie?' asked the man.

'He's the bloke who plants the trees.'

> **What holds the moon up in the sky?**
>
> Moonbeams!

Horace was wandering drunk through the street holding a dog's lead when he was stopped by a policeman who asked for his name.
'I'm not sure,' said Horace. 'You see, if I'm me, I've lost a dog. If I'm not me, I've found a lead.'

Julie: When I grow up, do you think my name will be in lights in theatres across the country?
Johnny: Only if you change your name to 'Emergency Exit'.

Horace: Where are you off to?
Herbert: To a surprise party for Sheila – weren't you invited?
Horace: No, but I'll come anyway – it'll be an even bigger surprise.

Horace: Do you know Raquel Welch is seventy-five!

Herbert: That's amazing, and she wasn't very well when she was born.

Horace: How do you know that?

Herbert: It said in the paper she was born in Chicago, ill.

Foreman: Horace! You're not supposed to smoke while you're working.

Horace: That's all right, I'm not working.

Horace: I've got a joke, I might have told you it before.

Herbert: Is it a funny one?

Horace: Oh yes.

Herbert: Then you haven't.

> **Have you heard about the new 'Divorced Barbie'?**
>
> It comes with all Ken's stuff.

> ## Where do you get a dead heat with only one entry?
>
> The crematorium.

Horace: My dog died after I gave him the powder you let me have.

Herbert: It was powerful stuff – are you sure you didn't give him too much?

Horace: No, I remembered you told me to give him no more than what would cover a two-pound coin – well, I didn't have a two-pound coin, so I had to use four 50p pieces instead.

Diner: What's this insect in my soup?

Waiter: Who do you think I am, David Attenborough?

Harriet: When we got married you said you'd spend your whole life trying to make me happy.

Horace: Yes, but I didn't expect to live this long.

A policeman was driving along the motorway when he overtook a car driven by a little old lady who was knitting. He wound down his window and shouted, 'Pull over!'
'No,' replied the old lady, 'it's a cardigan.'

Patient: How was that, doc?
Doctor: Very impressive, but I said I wanted to hear your *heart*?

Horace: Have you heard of that new website for learning ventriloquism?
Herbert: What's the address?
Horace: Guggle-yew, Guggle-yew, Guggle-yew, dot...

What do convicts use to talk to each other?

Cell phones!

> **Johnny: Dad's jokes aren't half-bad.**
>
> Julie: No, they're all bad.

Sally: I really hate it when my aunties and grannies come up to me at weddings and say, 'You're next!'
Susie: Well, you should do the same to them at funerals.

Teacher: Julie, what's a comet?
Julie: A star with a tail, sir.
Teacher: Correct. Johnny, can you name one?
Johnny: Er, Lassie?

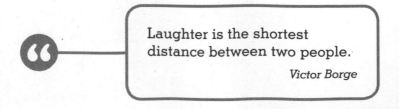

Laughter is the shortest distance between two people.
Victor Borge

Herbert and Horace were digging a ditch when Horace made a particularly careless swipe of his spade and cut off Herbert's ear.

'Help me find it in all this mud,' said Herbert, knowing that if it could be recovered it could be sewn back on – he wasn't stupid.

After a couple of minutes, Horace gave a triumphant shout, 'Here it is!'

'That's not it,' said Herbert, inspecting the ear. 'Mine had a pencil behind it.'

Horace: Last night someone painted 'NGAB' on my car.

Herbert: That's bang out of order, that is.

Who has a parrot that says, 'Pieces of two!'

Short John Silver.

> **What's got twelve legs, one eye and four tails?**
>
> Three blind mice and half a kipper.

What happened to the cow who got drunk?
Next day she had an awful hangunder.

Teacher: What sort of bird is a macaw?
Billy: Is it a Scottish crow, miss?

Publican: I had to throw out that bloke who played the baddie in *Skyfall* the other day.
Horace: Javier Bardem?
Publican: No, he can come back when he sobers up.

DAD STAT

1 in 8 Dads admit to breaking crockery deliberately in an attempt to get out of washing up.

Jimmy: What's your favourite Telly-Tubby?
Dad: Probably the Sony 42" flat-screen. And don't be so cheeky.

Horace: What are you doing with that old greyhound?
Herbert: I'm going to race it.
Horace: By the looks of it you'd probably beat it.

What do you call someone who lends tools to his neighbour?
A saw loser.

Horace: Why have you got a fried egg on your head?
Herbert: The boiled ones kept rolling off.

Why does Noddy wear a little hat with a bell on it?

Because he's a twit.

Dad's Daft Ditties
There was a young man called Perkins
    Who was simply addicted to gherkins.
He found them so nice,
But he ate too much spice,
    And pickled his internal workin's.

A treason plot has been uncovered among a group of blackcurrants.
The purple traitors have been arrested.

Horace: I've just had a letter from a Lancashire transvestite.
Herbert: How do you work that out?
Horace: Well, he had a Wigan address.

Horace: My Mum and Dad were called Pearl and Dean.
Herbert: Don't you mean your Ma and Pa-pa-pa-pa-pa-pa-pa-pa-pa-pa-pa?

What's the difference between jam and marmalade?

You can't get stuck in a traffic marmalade.

Teacher: What do we mean by a posthumous novel?

Jimmy: Is it one written after the author died, miss?

RE teacher: Jimmy, what's a Hindu?

Jimmy: Lay eggs, miss.

Who sits at a tractor shouting, 'The end is nigh!'?

Farmer Geddon.

Shaggy Dad Story #5

A knight was desperate to enter the big tournament but he hadn't got a horse. He told his page to find him something, anything, so he could enter the jousting. The page tried everywhere to find a horse, or even a pony, but there was nothing around. He tried a cow, but couldn't get the saddle on. He thought about a pig but none of them were tall enough.

Then someone told him there was a huge dog wandering around the common. 'That'll do,' he thought, and dashed off. He managed to catch the dog – it was huge, but it was a sorry sight. Nevertheless, the page was desperate, so he put a rope on it and took it back to the castle.

When he got there the steward was at the gate. 'What are you doing with that mutt?' he asked. The page explained.

'Look at it, though,' said the steward. 'It's flea-bitten, mangy, filthy. I don't care what he said …

'… You wouldn't send a knight out on a dog like this.'

> **There's been an explosion at a pie factory.**
> Police say there were 3.14 casualties.

Horace: I'm fed up of being told I have to change my password.
Herbert: It's a pain, isn't it?
Horace: Yes, I've had to rename my dog four times now.

What did the dyslexic man do when his house was plagued with poltergeists?
He called for goats' butter.

Customer: How much for a haircut?
Barber: Ten pounds.
Customer: And how much for a shave?
Barber: Five pounds.
Customer: Well, can you shave my head?

A duck was waiting to cross the road when a chicken came running up and said, 'Don't do it, you'll never hear the end of it.'

Doctor: How old are you?
Patient: In a month I'll be seventy.
Doctor: Oh – I hope you haven't planned a party.

Large lady on bus: If you were a gentleman, you'd get up and let one of these ladies sit down.
Man: Well, if you were a lady, you'd get up and let all of them sit down.

Why did Courtney Cox?

Because Lisa Kudrow.

What is a wally?

Something made out of brickies.

Did you hear about the Irishman who didn't get a job on a building site because he was too clever?
The foreman asked him the difference between 'joist' and 'girder' and the Irishman said, 'The first wrote *Ulysses* and the second wrote *Faust*.'

Horace and Herbert are riding a tandem up a long hill. Eventually they reach the top.
Herbert says, 'That was hard work.'
'Yes,' says Horace, 'and steep – if I hadn't had the brakes on I think we'd have rolled all the way back down.'

Teacher: Why are you late, Johnny?

Johnny: A man was looking for a twenty-pound note.

Teacher: And you were helping him?

Johnny: No, I was standing on it until he gave up.

Lawyer: My client will never get justice! Half of the judges in this country are crooks.

Judge: You must withdraw that remark.

Lawyer: Very well, my lord. Half of the judges in this country are *not* crooks.

Herbert: What would you do if I won the Lottery?

Harriet: I'd divorce you and take my half of the money.

Horace: Great, I've just won twenty quid – here's your tenner.

Sheila: I've got a model husband.

Joyce: Pity it's not a working model.

Herbert: It's taken me ages, but I've made a belt out of old watches.

Horace: That sounds like a waist of time.

Johnny: When I grow up I want to be a pop star.

Mum: Make your mind up, you can't do both.

A little boy was saying his prayers after his Gran had read him a story.

'God bless Mummy, Daddy and Gran, and PLEASE SEND ME A NEW BIKE FOR MY BIRTHDAY.'

'You don't need to shout, dear,' said his Gran, 'God isn't deaf.'

'No, Gran, but you are.'

> ## How does the chicken-pox charity raise money?
> With scratch cards.

An eight-foot-tall man went for a job as a lifeguard.

'First things first, can you swim?' he was asked.

'No, but I can't half wade.'

Doctor: I want you to take the green pill with a glass of water at breakfast, the blue pill with two glasses of water at lunchtime and the red pill with a glass of water each night.

Patient: So what's my problem?

Doctor: You're not drinking enough water.

Horace: That horse you put a bet on has turned round and is running in the wrong direction.

Herbert: That's OK, I backed it each way.

Parishioner: Vicar, your sermon today was like the peace and love of God.

Vicar: Thank you, why do you say that?

Parishioner: Because the peace of God passeth all understanding and the love of God endureth forever.

What's the difference between a musician and a large pizza?

A large pizza can feed a family of four.

Diner: Waiter, my salad's completely frozen.

Waiter: That'll be the iceberg lettuce, sir.

What are the simple instructions that make the Adam Ant diet so successful?

'Don't chew ever, don't chew ever.'

> **Why are boxing rings square?**

A vicar paid a decorator to whitewash the church, but he thinned his paint down so much that the first time it rained it all washed away. The vicar rang the decorator and complained.

'What do you want me to do about it?' asked the decorator.

'Repaint,' said the vicar, 'and thin no more.'

Customer in hardware shop: Have you got long nails?

Assistant: Yes, sir.

Customer: Great, can you scratch my back?

What did the stupid criminal say when he took part in an identity parade?

'That's him!'

What did the cowboy say to the German car?

Audi!

> **Who cleans windows as he sings?**
>
> Shammy Davis Jr.

Doctor: I see you've married a much younger woman.
Herbert: Well, you told me to 'get a hot momma and be cheerful'.
Doctor: I told you you'd got a heart murmur and to be careful!

Horace: Did you say I bring happiness wherever I go?
Harriet: No, I said *when*ever you go.

Examiner: When driving through fog, what should you use?
Herbert: Your car.

Customer: I've had to come in to see you because you never answer the phone.

Assistant: What number have you been dialling, sir?

Customer: The one on your website – 0800 1800.

Assistant: They're our opening hours.

Slade re-formed and were going on *Top of the Pops*. Noddy Holder was being helped into his stage costume.

'Flared trousers, Noddy?'

'Lovely, ta.'

'Mirror hat, Noddy?'

'Lovely, ta.'

'Nearly done. Kipper tie, Noddy?'

'Lovely, two sugars, ta.'

What happened to the lazy campers?

They were charged with loitering within tent.

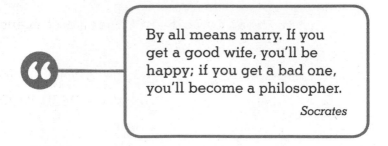

By all means marry. If you get a good wife, you'll be happy; if you get a bad one, you'll become a philosopher.

Socrates

A burglar has stolen all the light bulbs from the local police station.

Police say they are completely in the dark.

There are reports of big holes in the lawn in front of MI6's headquarters.

Everything points to them having a mole.

Bobby: Dad, I'm in the school orchestra playing the triangle.

Dad: Well, that'll give you some ting to do.

Patient: Doctor, everyone thinks I'm a liar.

Doctor: I don't believe you.

Sheila: Can I try on that dress in the window?
Assistant: If you like, but most people use the changing rooms.

Horace: My wife's not very happy.
Herbert: Why's that then?
Horace: She said she wanted an animal coat for her birthday so I got her a donkey jacket.

Patient: So, have I got an inferiority complex, doctor?
Doctor: No, not at all. You really are inferior.

What do you give a forgetful cow?

Milk of amnesia.

Dad's Daft Ditties

A chap who was on the decline
    Stuck his head on the railway line,
But he died of ennui
As the 4.23
    Didn't come till a quarter to nine.

**Sheila: I want to complain about my room –
I can see the man in the house across the
street undressing.**
Landlord: But you can't see his bedroom
window from here.
Sheila: I can if I climb on top of the wardrobe.

**Horace: Why are you swimming backstroke all
the time?**
Herbert: I've just had my lunch and I don't want
to swim on a full stomach.

> **Why was the toothpaste late?**
>
> It got held up in the Tube!

Barrister: Isn't it correct, Mr Smith, that after the crash my client asked you if you were all right and you said you were?

Smith: Up to a point.

Barrister: What do you mean, up to a point?

Smith: Well, I was riding my horse and cart with my dog in the back when his car hit us. He went up to my horse and said, 'Oh, his leg's broken, poor thing,' and shot it. Then he went up to my dog and said, 'Massive internal bleeding, poor thing,' and shot it. Then he came up to me and asked if I was all right …

DAD STAT

The average Dad has £45 worth of unused gym membership.

Why has Keith Chegwin
given up alcohol?

Because Cheggers can't be boozers!

Horace: Do you still go to watch your local football team?
Herbert: Yes, but there are so few of us, before kick-off they announce the names of the crowd to the players.

Horace: My Granddad died at exactly 3:45 and at precisely the same time his grandfather clock stopped.
Herbert: That's amazing.
Horace: Well, not really. That's when it fell on top of him.

Harry Potter's been having trouble with his wand, and since the repairer added lots of attachments it's got worse. It will now only cast a spell that makes people support a Lancashire football team. Bolt-on Wand-Errors.

If a buttercup is yellow, what colour is a hiccup?

Burple.

There were two flies on a bald man's head.
One says to the other: 'I remember when this was a footpath.'

Teacher: Complete the saying, 'If at first you don't succeed ...'
Jimmy: Destroy all the evidence that you tried.

Two prehistoric men were standing by Stonehenge. One says to the other:
'I can remember when all this was fields...'

Horace: I read the other day that beer was bad for you, so I'm giving it up.
Herbert: What, you're giving up beer?
Horace: No, I'm giving up reading.

Horace: We've paid a fortune to fish here and only caught two.
Herbert: Yes, each fish has cost us £80.
Horace: Well, if you put it like that, it's a good job we didn't catch any more.

> **What did the little mountain say to the big mountain?**
>
> Hi, Cliff!

Horace and Harriet were in their hotel room when the fire alarm went off. Harriet opened the door but the corridor was full of smoke.
'We'll have to jump out of the window,' said Horace.
'But we're on the thirteenth floor,' pointed out Harriet.
'This is no time to be superstitious!'

Customer: Hello, I'd like to book a room for next week. Is it right you're a stone's throw from the beach?
Hotelier: Yes sir.
Customer: Lovely, and are you easy to find?
Hotelier: Yes, we're the one with the broken windows.

**Horace: I don't think much of this dictionary
I bought.**

Herbert: Why not?

Horace: Well, it hasn't got an index for a start.

**After being out all weekend on a bender, Horace
finally came home on Monday morning to find
Harriet waiting for him.**

'How would you like it if you didn't see me for a
couple of days?' she asked.

'Suits me,' replied Horace.

Well, he didn't see her for the rest of Monday, or
Tuesday, or Wednesday, but by Thursday morning
the swelling had gone down enough that he could
just see a little bit out of the corner of one eye …

Who is sticky and sings?

Gluey Armstrong.

> **Where's the most common place to get mugged?**
>
> At the cosh point.

First student: I copied my essay on the Black Death from the Internet.
Second student: Does that make you a bubonic plagiarist?

Two convicts were about to be executed and were asked if they had any last requests.
The first said he'd like to hear his favourite One Direction song for the last time.
The second asked if he could be killed first.

Jimmy: What has having kids taught you, Dad?
Dad: I suppose it's taught me patience, tolerance, self-denial, and lots of other things I wouldn't have needed if I hadn't had kids.

Four students went to a great party, overslept and missed an exam the next morning. They agreed to tell their professor they'd travelled in together and had a puncture on the way in that morning, which had caused them to be late, and asked if they could sit the exam the next day. The professor agreed.

The next morning they sat down and turned over the exam paper. It read: 'This exam consists of one question, worth 100 per cent. Which tyre had the puncture?'

11.3 – the average number of balls the neighbours throw back in autumn when everything's died back.

DAD STAT

A woman approached a man in the pub thinking he'd been on *The Apprentice*, when in fact he'd appeared on *Big Brother*.

Police say it was a case of mistaken non-entity.

A rambler was walking through the countryside when he saw a farmer holding a pig up to an apple tree while the pig ate the apples off it.

'Excuse me,' said the rambler, 'but wouldn't it be a lot quicker if you just shook the apples onto the floor.'

'Maybe,' said the farmer, 'but time's nothing to a pig.'

What's big and white and goes up and down?

A bi-polar bear.

> **What dog has no head?**
>
> A King Charles the First spaniel.

What do you get if you cross a vacuum cleaner with a door-to-door evangelist?
A Jehoover's Witness!

What did one Dalek say to the other?
I've seen twelve different doctors now and none of them have had a clue what's wrong with me.

How does Dick Dastardly find his way around?
With his Double Drat-nav.

Doctor: I think your best bet is to go abroad for treatment.
Patient: Have you got anywhere specific in mind?
Doctor: I'd try Lourdes if I was you.

Horace: I've taken up boxing but had to have a medical; when the results came back my trainer said I'd got sugar diabetes.
Herbert: Great, when do you fight him?

What do you call it when someone plays 'Waterloo' on a didgeridoo?
Abbariginal!

What's got four legs, an udder and can see just as well from both ends?
A cow with its eyes shut.

Lawyer: And what made you think it was my client that crashed into the shop, officer?
Policeman: I found the 'eavy-dents on 'is car, sir.

What do you get if you divide the circumference of an apple by its radius?

Apple pi!

> **What do you call a fawn with a machine gun?**
>
> Bambo.

Teacher: What family does the platypus belong to, Jimmy?
Jimmy: I don't think anyone in our street's got one, sir.
Sally: Mummy, why do you keep poking Daddy in the ribs?
Mum: I don't want the fire to go out.

Horace: It's very dark tonight, isn't it?
Herbert: I don't know, I can't see a flippin' thing.

Paratrooper: What happens if my parachute doesn't open?
Sergeant: Bring it back and we'll give you a new one.

> **Passenger: Do you stop at the Ritz?**
> Bus driver: What, on my wages?

Horace: I see those two lavatory attendants got married.
Herbert: Yes, but I think it's just a marriage of convenience.

A large amount of hay has gone missing from some stables.
Police are making horse-to-horse enquiries.

Dad's Daft Ditties
There was an old man of Japan
    Whose limericks didn't quite scan.
When folk asked him why,
He replied, 'It's cause I
    Always try to fit as many words
    into the last line as I can.'

> **Mum: How did your first day at school go?**
>
> Susie: Not very well – I've got to go back tomorrow.

What did the man win for coming second in a Patrick Moore lookalike competition?
A constellation prize!

Horace: Congratulations on your baby, Herbert. Is it a boy or a girl?
Herbert: Of course it is!

Why did the mean jockey buy just one spur?
He reckoned if he could get one side of the horse to go faster the other side would follow.

What's the best invention ever?
Window blinds – if it weren't for them it'd be curtains for everyone!

> **Customer: Why did you become a butcher?**
>
> Butcher: Because I like meating people.

Herbert's son went to university and after three years phoned his Dad to say he'd got his BA.
'Great,' said Herbert, 'only twenty-four letters to go – and try and get the rest of them in the right order!'

Teacher: Tommy, you're late. Don't you have an alarm clock?
Tommy: Yes, miss, but it went off while I was asleep.

Mum: Do you think Roger is doing his best at school?
Teacher: Yes, I'm afraid he is.

Teacher: What can you tell me about the Dead Sea?
Billy: I didn't even know it had been ill.

Dad's Charts

Typical Dad's idea of a pie chart:

■ Meat and potato
□ Steak and kidney
■ Apple and blackcurrant

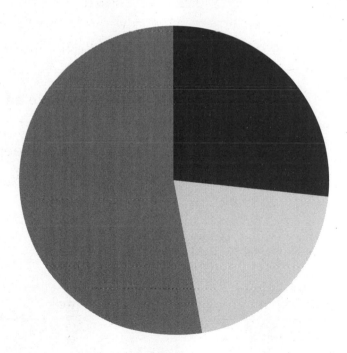

There's been an explosion at the factory that paints pillar boxes — a man is missing presumed red.

Mum: Why did you put a spider in your sister's bed?
Billy: Because I couldn't find a wasp.

Teacher: Jimmy, I'm not going to tell you to stop talking again.
Jimmy: Thank you, miss.

Shaggy Dad Story #6

Stevie Wonder was doing a concert and towards the end he decided to ask for requests.

One man shouted out, 'Play a jazz chord!'

It was a strange request, but simple enough, so Stevie played a cool chord on the piano.

'No,' shouted the man, 'a jazz chord!'

Puzzled, Stevie tried another more complicated chord, but got the same response. He tried again and again, until he was playing chords he'd never done before his life. Still the man wasn't satisfied.

'No,' he insisted, 'a jazz chord. You know …

'"A jazz chord to say I love you".'

19 – The average number of concerts and nativity plays Dad will have to attend during the school life of one child.

Patient: Doctor, I keep thinking I'm a lift.
Doctor: Sounds like you're just coming down with something.

Horace: My wife was digging up some carrots yesterday and tore her hamstring.
Herbert: What did you do?
Horace: I opened a tin of peas.

What did the sea monster say when it saw the submarine?
Oh no, tinned food again!

Tarzan: I'm not feeling very well.

Doctor: Oh dear, say 'Aaaaaaaaaaaaaahhhhhhhhhh!'

> $F(x)$ walks into a bar and asks for a sandwich. The landlord says, 'I'm sorry, we don't cater for functions.'

How do you know when your house is nearly full of toadstools?

There won't be mushroom inside.

Billy: Do you know when Harry's birthday is?

Bobby: No, but I think it's sometime this year.

Did you hear that Oxygen and Magnesium have got together?

OMG!

Solicitor: Twenty pounds to cut my hair – but I'm nearly bald!

Barber: Yes, there was a £15 search fee.

What do you call an Australian prophet who absorbs the Ten Commandments?

Oz-Moses.

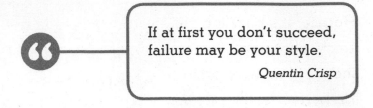

If at first you don't succeed,
failure may be your style.

Quentin Crisp

Why was Jason Orange asked to leave Take That?
He couldn't concentrate.

**Statistics teacher: Every time I breathe out,
someone dies.**
Charlie: Have you tried antiseptic mouthwash, sir?

**What dresses in robes and runs through the
desert with a bedpan and a lamp?**
Florence of Arabia.

**Customer: Why haven't
you got any ice cubes here?**

Barman: The chap with the
recipe took another job.

Horace: It's puzzling me, every day when I get to my allotment, someone's spread a couple of inches of manure on it.
Herbert: Aha, the plot thickens.

Customer: Can I have those ten-pound earrings for my wife, please, and gift-wrap them.
Assistant: Is it a surprise?
Customer: Yes, she's expecting a diamond necklace.

A lorry-load of Vick's Sinex nasal spray has overturned on the M25.
Police say there will be no congestion for twelve hours.

Patient: Nurse, can I have a bedpan please?
Nurse: Sorry, I'm the head nurse.

Sheila: Have you noticed I bought a new toilet brush?
Frank: Yes, I tried it, but I think I prefer paper.

Customer: I'll have a bar of soap, please.
Chemist: Certainly, sir, would you like it scented?
Customer: No, I'll take it with me.

Horace: I tried to catch the fog yesterday.
Herbert: What happened?
Horace: Mist!

Horace: Have you ever been unfaithful to your wife?
Herbert: No, I love my house far too much to do that.

Horace: What do you think of wind turbines?

Herbert: I'm a big fan.

> **What do you call a magic dog?**
>
> A Labracadabrador.

Diner: I'll have the fish – wait, I tell you what, make it a steak and kidney pie.
Waiter: The chef's not a magician, sir.

How many men does it take to change a toilet roll?
Nobody knows, it's never happened.

Joyce: I know I shouldn't have married a tennis player.
Sheila: Why?
Joyce: Love means nothing to him.

Preacher: Do you know what you must do before your sins are forgiven?
Member of congregation: Sin!

Horace: Why is your son's band called 999 megabytes?
Herbert: They still haven't got a gig.

Frank: Let's go out tonight.
Sheila: Curry OK?
Frank: No, I want to eat, not sing.

Does Saudi Arabian TV show *The Flintstones*?
No, but Abu Dhabi do!

Horace: I haven't slept for five days.
Herbert: Well, neither have I ...
that would be far too long.

If a fire hydrant has H_2O on the inside, what does it have on the outside?
K9P.

92 per cent of Dads have refereed a football match their child has been playing in – 2 per cent have done it more than once.

DAD STAT

Horace: I know you've been to the dentist, but what are those high notes coming from inside your mouth?
Herbert: That's my falsetto teeth.

Doctor: It seems you've got pantomime syndrome.
Patient: Oh no I haven't.

What's the most insignificant animal in the jungle?

An irrelephant.

Big Ted: Do you want some pudding?

Little Ted: No, I'm stuffed.